*From Your Friends At* **The MAILBOX®**

# SEPTEMBER

## A MONTH OF REPRODUCIBLES AT YOUR FINGERTIPS!

**Grades 2–3**

D1405641

### Project Editor:
Amy Erickson

### Editor:
Darcy Brown

### Writers:
Darcy Brown, Amy Erickson, Allison White Haynes,
Cynthia Holcomb, Nicole Iacovazzi, Laura Mihalenki
Kimberly Taylor

### Art Coordinator:
Clevell Harris

### Artists:
Jennifer Tipton Bennett, Nick Greenwood, Clevell Harris,
Susan Hodnett, Sheila Krill, Kimberly Richard,
Rebecca Saunders, Donna K. Teal

### Cover Artist:
Jennifer Tipton Bennett

©1999 by THE EDUCATION CENTER, INC.
All rights reserved.
ISBN #1-56234-267-3

**Manufactured in the United States**
10 9 8 7 6 5 4 3 2 1

# Table Of Contents

**September Calendar** .................................................................. 3
Activities for free-time learning fun.

**Events And Activities For The Family** ...................................... 4
Three events and activities for families and students to explore at home.

**Back To School** ........................................................................ 5
Leap into a new school year with these "toad-ily" terrific ideas!

**Labor Day** ................................................................................ 11
Honor workers and recognize students for jobs well done with this
Labor Day unit.

**Simply Grand!** ......................................................................... 15
Celebrate Grandparents Day with this creative collection of activities
and reproducibles.

**It's Apple Time!** ...................................................................... 19
This apple unit is packed with bushels of skill-based ideas.

**Autumn** .................................................................................... 25
Harvest this bountiful crop of autumn activities and reproducibles.

**Tomie dePaola** ........................................................................ 31
These literature-based activities are perfect for celebrating author
Tomie dePaola's September birthday.

**National Student Day™** ........................................................... 35
Spotlight students with this "dino-mite" collection of activities, reproducibles,
and awards.

**All Eyes On Owls** .................................................................... 39
Learn about the fascinating world of owls with these informative ideas.

**All-American Breakfast Month** ................................................ 45
This appetizing unit is made-to-order for a hearty helping of learning fun!

**Ice Cream Month** ..................................................................... 49
Get the scoop on this tasty treat with these mouthwatering ideas.

**National Chicken Month** .......................................................... 55
This chicken-related unit is filled with "eggs-cellent" activities and
reproducibles.

**National Honey Month** ............................................................. 59
This sweet tribute to honey is sure to tickle your students' taste buds!

**Answer Keys** ........................................................................... 63

# September Free Time

| Monday | Tuesday | Wednesday | Thursday | Friday |
|--------|---------|-----------|----------|--------|
| Labor Day (the first Monday in September) honors working people. List five workers who helped you last week. Write a sentence about each one.  | September 2, 1789, marks the date when Congress established the U.S. Treasury Department. Draw a new design for the one-dollar bill.  | September is All-American Breakfast Month. Write a paragraph describing your favorite breakfast foods. 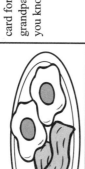 | Grandparents Day is celebrated on the first Sunday after Labor Day. Make a special card for a grandparent you know.  | This month is National Courtesy Month. Write a thank-you note to a person who has helped you at school. Thank You |
| Anna Mary Moses, also known as Grandma Moses, was born on September 7, 1860. She began a painting career at the age of 76. Paint a picture in honor of this artist. | Write a list of ten autumn words. Beside each word, write how many syllables it has.  2 football  1 rake  2 pumpkin | If you had 50 cents, what coins could you have? Write three different answers.  | Orville Wright made a famous airplane flight on September 9, 1908. If you could fly anywhere, where would you fly and why? Write your answer. 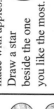 | The first newspaper cartoon strip was published on September 11, 1875. Draw a comic strip about your school. |
| Milton Hershey, founder of the famous Hershey candy company, was born on September 13, 1857. Design a label for a new candy bar.  CANDY BAR | Write the words "September Free Time" on a sheet of paper. Write as many words as you can, using only the letters in these words.  *pet*  *rest*  *meet* | On September 14, 1902, the first teddy bear was created in honor of President Teddy Roosevelt. Design and label a new kind of teddy bear on a sheet of drawing paper. | The Pilgrims left Plymouth, England, on September 16, 1620. Pretend you were a Pilgrim on the ship. Write a journal entry about your trip.  | The first successful gasoline-powered car in America was driven on September 21, 1893. Write a story about what life would be like without cars. |
| Autumn begins on September 22 or 23. List ten things that you like to do in the fall.  | Johann Galle, a German astronomer, discovered the planet Neptune on September 23, 1846. Write the names of the other eight planets. 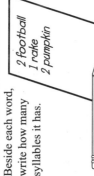 | Famous folk hero Johnny Appleseed was born on September 26, 1774. Make a list of five foods that are made with apples. Draw a star beside the one you like the most.  | The fourth Sunday in September is National Good Neighbor Day. Write about one way you can be a good neighbor. | Write the numerals from 0 to 102 by 3s. Then circle each odd number.  0,3,6,9 |

**Note To The Teacher:** Have each student staple a copy of this page inside a file folder. Direct students to store their completed work in their folders.

# September
## Events And Activities For The Family

**Directions:** Select at least one activity below to complete as a family by the end of September.
*(Challenge: See if your family can complete all three activities.)*

### International Literacy Day

Promote reading and writing in your family by celebrating International Literacy Day on September 8. Visit your local library and check out some books by favorite children's authors who have September birthdays, such as the ones shown. Read the selected books together. Then ask each family member to write and share a paragraph about his or her favorite book. If desired, make this a weekly family activity. Now that's a great way to make reading and writing a family affair!

### All-American Breakfast Month

Celebrate All-American Breakfast Month to emphasize the importance of eating a nutritious breakfast. Ask your family to brainstorm breakfast foods they enjoy eating, and write their responses on a large sheet of paper. Then enlist the help of family members to draw a happy face beside each nutritious food and a sad face beside each food that is not healthful. Explain that it is important to eat a healthful breakfast every day, and post the list in a convenient location as a reminder. Using the list as a reference, have each family member help plan and prepare at least one nutritious breakfast this month.

### Birthday Of Jim Henson

Jim Henson, well-known puppeteer and creator of the Muppets®, was born in Mississippi on September 24, 1936. He received numerous awards for the puppets he designed for productions such as "Sesame Street"® and "The Muppet Show." Celebrate the life of this creative performer by inviting your family members to become puppeteers. Provide old socks (or paper bags) and a variety of craft items for family members to use to create their own unique puppets. Then have them write and perform puppet shows for one another.

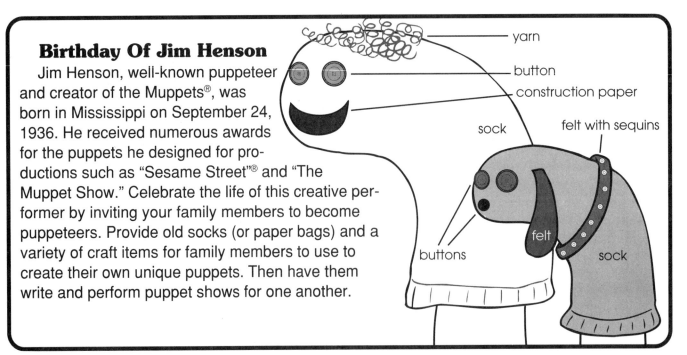

# Back To School

Leap into a new school year with these "toad-ily" terrific ideas!

## Personalized Posters

Learn more about the students in your "pad" as they complete these personalized back-to-school posters. Give each student a copy of page 6. Have each student illustrate her sheet with pictures of her family, friends, home, and hobbies as indicated. Next instruct her to glue her sheet atop a slightly larger sheet of colored construction paper. Have her use markers to write her name across the top of the construction paper. If desired, ask each student to create a decorative back-to-school border around her resulting poster. Encourage each youngster to share her work with the class. Then collect the completed posters, and display them on a bulletin board titled "Meet The Students In Our Pad!"

## Pond Puzzler

This pond puzzler is sure to provide your youngsters with plenty of number-sequencing practice! Duplicate one copy of the reproducible on page 8 for each student. Explain to your students that they will be helping Tammy Toad get out of the pond. To help her find the path, have each youngster place his pencil on the smallest number on the pond *(1)*. Next ask each student to draw a line to the next greatest number directly above, below, or beside the first number *(4)*. Have him continue in the same manner until Tammy Toad reaches the exit. Then instruct him to write on the lines, in order, each number he used. To provide additional practice with sequencing numbers, challenge each student to complete the Bonus Box activity.

## Tic-Tac-Toad

Challenge your students to practice their addition skills with this exciting variation of tic-tac-toe. Pair students; then provide each pair with a copy of the gameboard on page 7. Direct each twosome to cut out the number cards at the bottom of their sheet and place them facedown next to the gameboard. To play, each student, in turn, picks up a card and places it faceup in a square of his choice. Play continues until the sum of three numbers in any direction equals 15 (a Tic-Tac-Toad), or until all of the numbers have been used. If a player's sum equals 15, he is declared the winner. If a sum of 15 is not reached, the game is a draw and a new game begins. Have students continue play until game time is over. If desired, hold weekly Tic-Tac-Toad tournaments to determine a class champion!

Name _____

# All About Me!

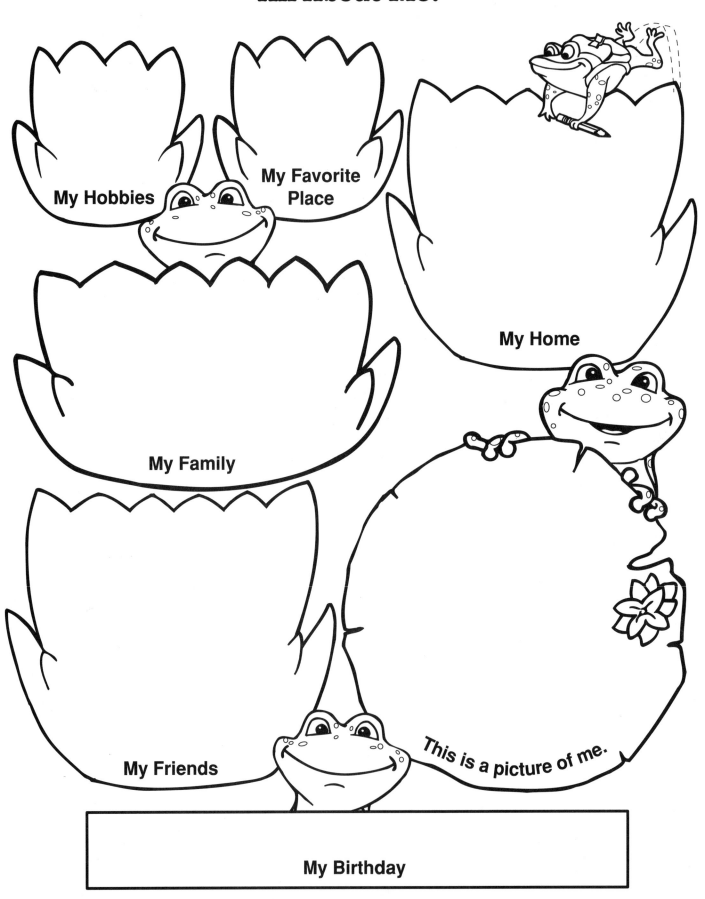

My Hobbies

My Favorite Place

My Home

My Family

My Friends

This is a picture of me.

My Birthday

# Tic-Tac-Toad

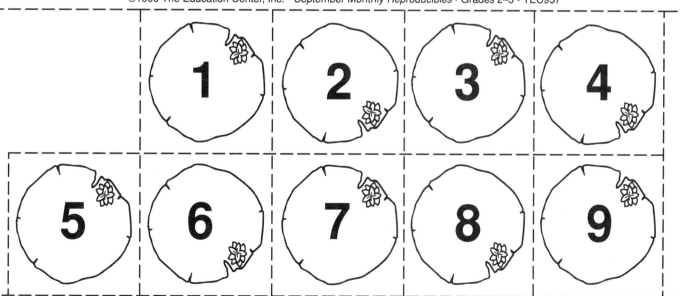

**Note To The Teacher:** Use with "Tic-Tac-Toad" on page 5.

# Pond Puzzler

Tammy Toad needs your help to get out of the pond.
Follow your teacher's directions to help Tammy.

EXIT

| 53 | 99 | 82 | 88 | 94 |
| 48 | 26 | 75 | 71 | 15 |
| 7 | 14 | 66 | 70 | 64 |
| 26 | 35 | 39 | 44 | 55 |
| 11 | 43 | 52 | 47 | 50 |
| 4 | 1 | 16 | 3 | 97 |

START

___ ___ ___ ___ ___ ___ ___ ___

___ ___ ___ ___ ___ ___ ___

**Bonus Box:** Write the numbers that Tammy didn't hop on in order from *greatest* to *least* on the back of this sheet.

# Welcome To Our Pad!

Write each back-to-school word in the correct spaces.

bell        bike        desk
lunch       pencil      playground
school      student     math
books       teacher

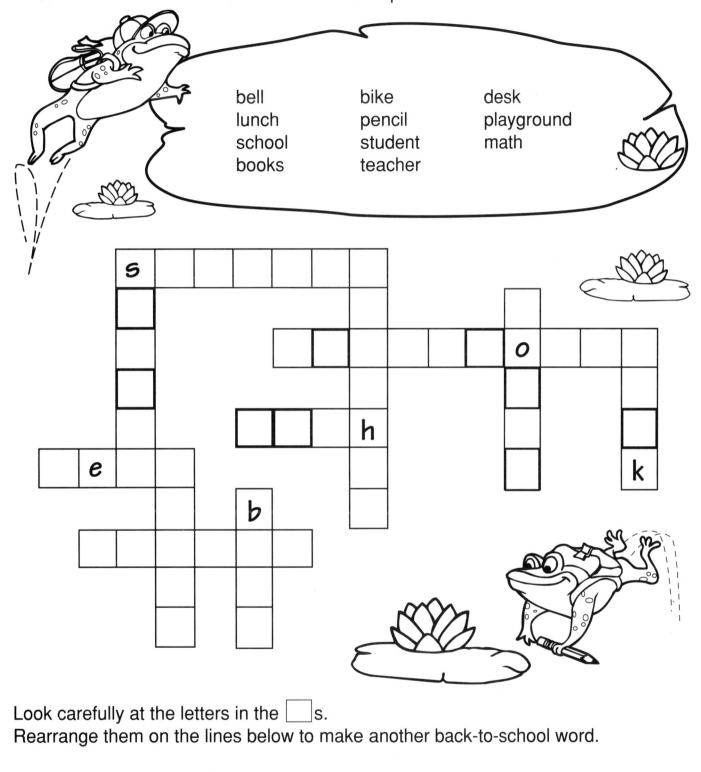

Look carefully at the letters in the ☐ s.
Rearrange them on the lines below to make another back-to-school word.

___ ___ ___ ___ ___ ___ ___

**Bonus Box:** Choose five back-to-school words. Draw and label a picture for each one on the back of this sheet.

# Hop! Hop! Hop!

Cut out and read each group of words.
If the words make a complete sentence, glue the cutout on the lily pad.

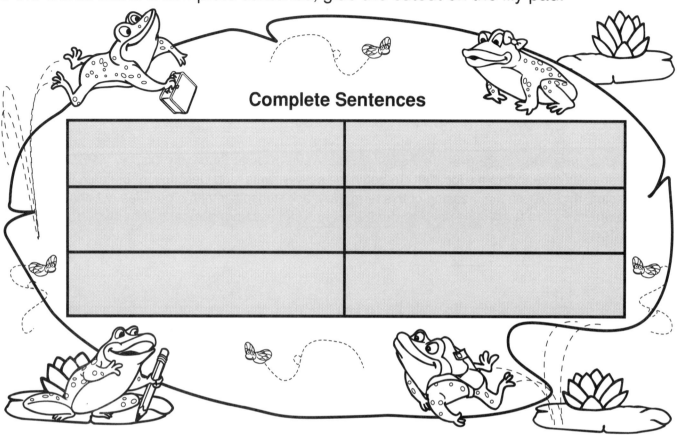

**Complete Sentences**

| | |
|---|---|
| Flies are buzzing everywhere. | Three toads hop to school. |
| One toad is carrying books. | Tom Toad is carrying his bookbag on his back. |
| The toads will learn at school. | The toads. |
| It is a sunny. | One toad brought his lunch. |
| One toad is. | The toads are happy because. |

# LABOR DAY

In the United States and Canada, Labor Day is observed on the first Monday in September. This holiday, set aside to honor working people, is the perfect time to celebrate the achievements and efforts of your little workers.

## Help Wanted

Here's a whole-group activity that's sure to remind your students that they're workers, too! In advance, prepare a poster with the heading "Help Wanted: Great Students!" Display the poster in a prominent and accessible location. To begin the activity, write "Job Description" beneath the heading, and explain the meaning of this term. Next ask students to name qualities or behaviors that are important for being a good student. List each response on the poster. When you observe a student demonstrating an advertised trait, acknowledge her for a job well done. Keep the poster on display throughout the year to remind youngsters that it is their "job" to do their best!

## It Takes All Kinds

Put some personality into your Labor Day activities with this one-of-a-kind art project! Begin by asking your students to think of careers that require special clothing or equipment. Then provide each youngster with a tagboard paper-doll cutout and a variety of craft materials, such as construction paper, fabric scraps, buttons, yarn, ribbon, and wiggle eyes. Invite each child to use the materials to outfit his figure for the career of his choice. Provide time for youngsters to share their completed projects with the class. Then collect the projects, and display them on a bulletin board titled "It Takes All Kinds."

## All Play, No Work

Balance work and play with a new twist on an old favorite—charades! Divide the class into two teams: A and B. Invite a player from Team A to come to the front of the room. Whisper a career to him, using the lists below as a reference if desired. Then ask him to pantomime it for the class. Allow his teammates one minute to guess his career. If Team A guesses correctly, award it one point. If the team can also tell whether this worker provides a good or a service, award it an additional point. If Team A does not guess correctly, Team B has an opportunity to try. Repeat the activity with Team B. Continue play until each child has had a chance to pantomime.

Workers Who
Provide Services
baseball pitcher
firefighter
hairstylist
teacher
waiter/waitress
bus driver
ballet dancer
rock star

Workers Who
Provide Goods
farmer
baker
lumberjack
pizza maker
seamstress
tailor
fisherman

11

**Interview Form**

Name of interviewer: _____

Name of person interviewed: _____

# A Worker's Words

Interview a grown-up you know well.
Write his or her answers on the lines.

1. What is your job? _____
   _____

2. What jobs, if any, did you have before this one? Please include jobs you had
   when you were a child.

   _____        _____

   _____        _____

   _____        _____

3. What responsibilities do you have at your job? _____
   _____

4. What do you like best about your job? _____

5. What do you like least about your job? _____

6. What is the hardest part of your job? _____

7. Do you need any special tools or training to do your job? Please explain.
   _____
   _____

8. What advice would you give someone who would like to have a job like yours?
   _____
   _____

Thank you.

**Note To The Teacher:** Once students have a good understanding of the meaning of Labor Day, invite them to interview a grown-up who
holds a job. Duplicate one copy of this page for each student. Instruct him to interview a grown-up he knows well. Then ask him to share his
results and write a report about what he learned.

Name _____

# Labor Day Lowdown

Read each sentence.
If it is a **fact**, color the circle in the fact column.
If it is an **opinion**, color the circle in the opinion column.

## HAPPY LABOR DAY !

| Fact | Opinion | |
|------|---------|---|
| J | W | 1. Labor Day is celebrated the first Monday in September. |
| I | Q | 2. Labor Day is a fun holiday. |
| N | D | 3. There are many different kinds of jobs. |
| G | B | 4. A firefighter's job is exciting. |
| X | T | 5. A librarian works with books. |
| A | K | 6. It is fun for teachers to work with children. |
| S | V | 7. A doctor's job is more important than a nurse's job. |
| L | P | 8. The president's job is harder than any other job. |
| U | R | 9. Some workers provide goods, and some workers provide services. |
| C | Y | 10. Bakers provide goods like cakes and cookies. |
| M | E | 11. A hairstylist provides a service. |
| F | H | 12. Workers are different in many ways, but they all love Labor Day. |

Now solve the riddle by cracking the code.
For each number, write the letter that is **not** colored.

Why doesn't anyone want the cannon's job?

___ ___    ___ ___ ___ ___ ___ ___
 2   5      6   8   1   6  10   7

___ ___ ___ ___    ___ ___ ___ ___ ___ !
 4  11   5   7     12   2   9  11   3

# All In A Day's Work

Cut out the clocks, and arrange them in order by time.
Put a drop of glue on each ●.
Glue the clocks in order along the trail.
Then write the time below each clock.

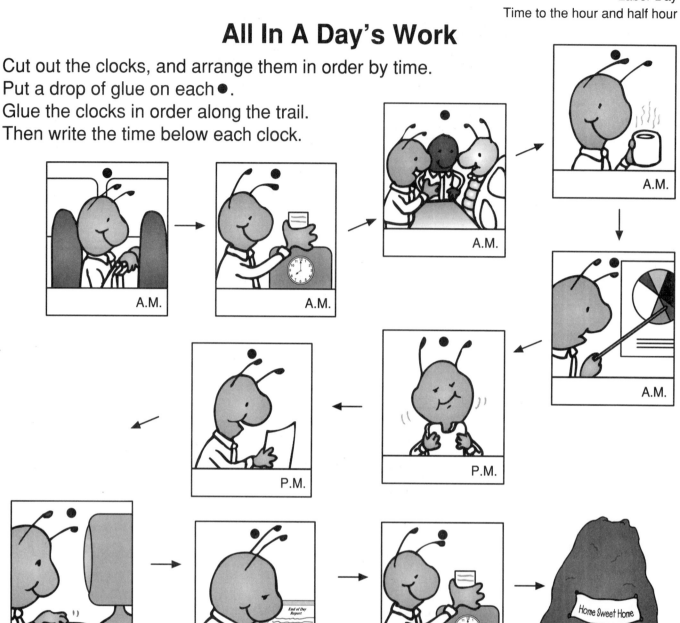

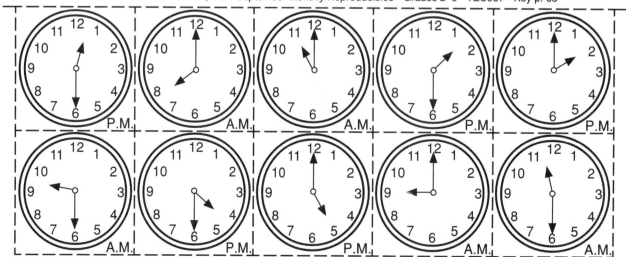

14

# SIMPLY GRAND!

The first Sunday after Labor Day is National Grandparents Day—a special time to show appreciation for elders. With this creative collection of ideas and reproducibles, youngsters can honor grandparents and other senior citizens in grand style!

## Three Cheers For Grandparents

Hip, hip, hooray! It's Grandparents Day! These student-made cards have a spirited message that is sure to bring lots of smiles to honored grandparents. Discuss with youngsters how each grandparent is different and is special in his or her own way. Have students share with the class some of the things that make their grandparents unique. Then give each student a copy of page 16. (If desired, provide additional copies for youngsters who would like to make a card for more than one grandparent.) On each page, a student writes something special about his grandparent. He colors each page and personalizes the last one. Then the youngster cuts out the pages. Next he accordion-folds a 6" x 18" strip of brightly colored construction paper into four equal sections (see the illustration). He decorates the front of the resulting card as desired. He opens the card, then sequences and glues the completed pages onto it. After the glue has dried, he folds the card again and presents it to his grandparent.

## Grand Introductions

Feature grandparents and senior friends with this biographical bulletin-board idea! Ask each student to draw and color a portrait of a grandparent or senior friend on an 8 1/2" x 11" sheet of paper. Next tell each student that she will write a biography of this person. Explain to youngsters that a biography is a factual story about someone's life. Have students brainstorm types of information that they could include in their biographies, such as where the person lives and his or her hobbies, likes, and dislikes. Record students' ideas on the chalkboard. Then, on a separate sheet of paper, have each youngster write a biography of her grandparent or senior friend, referring to the brainstormed list as she works. Have her staple her portrait and completed biography on a 12" x 18" sheet of colored construction paper. Give each youngster an opportunity to share her work with classmates; then display students' portraits and stories on a brightly colored bulletin board titled "Grand Introductions."

Grandma Bartlett

Grandma Bartlett lives next door. She is my dad's mom. Grandma works in an office.

Gramps

Gramps lives in Maine. He is 60 years old and has three kids. One of his kids is my mom! Gramps is a doctor. He loves to work in the garden on the weekends.

## Recommended Literature

*Grandpa's Garden Lunch* by Judith Caseley (Greenwillow Books, 1990)

*Shoes From Grandpa* by Mem Fox (Orchard Books, 1992)

*Wilfrid Gordon McDonald Partridge* by Mem Fox (Kane/Miller Book Publishers, 1989)

# Three Cheers For Grandparents!

Hip, Hip, Hooray!

©1999 The Education Center, Inc.

1 is for _____

_____

_____

2 is for _____

_____

_____

3 is for _____

_____

_____

Love,

©1999 The Education Center, Inc. • *September Monthly Reproducibles* • Grades 2–3 • TEC957

16    **Note To The Teacher:** Use with "Three Cheers For Grandparents" on page 15.

Name _____

Simply Grand!
Reading a map

# Grandma's Neighborhood

Use the key to read the map.
Answer the questions.

1. Is Grandma's house east or west of the restaurant? _____

2. Is Grandma's house closer to the forest or the mountains? _____

3. Is Hillview Street east or west of Grandma's house? _____

4. Is the park north or south of Grandma's house? _____

5. What streets should Grandma take to visit the school? _____
_____

6. Grandma is at the lake. What streets should she take to go home? _____
_____

**Bonus Box:** On the back of this sheet, write directions for Grandma to go from the school to the hospital.

©1999 The Education Center, Inc. • *September Monthly Reproducibles* • Grades 2–3 • TEC957 • Key p. 63    17

# A Letter From Grandpa

Read the letter.
Draw a box around each letter that should be capitalized.
Write the capital letter above the box.

dear emily,

    thank you for the grandparents day card. the picture you

drew is beautiful!

    today i took daisy to the park to play fetch. daisy got so

tired that she took a long nap when we got home!

    i'm glad that you are coming to visit in november. will it

be your first time on an airplane?

             love,

             grandpa

Answer the questions.

1. How did Grandpa let Emily know that he liked the card? _____

   _____

2. Who do you think Daisy is? Explain your answer. _____

   _____

3. Do you think Grandpa lives close to Emily? Why or why not? _____

   _____

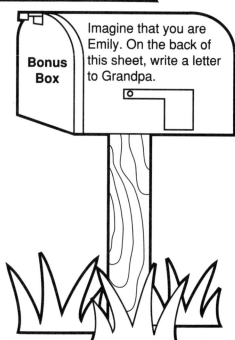

Bonus Box

Imagine that you are Emily. On the back of this sheet, write a letter to Grandpa.

**Note To The Teacher:** If desired, introduce this activity by reading aloud *Dear Annie* by Judith Caseley (Mulberry Books, 1994).

# It's Apple Time!

Get ready for bushels of excitement with this bumper crop of apple-related activities and reproducibles!

## Munching On Estimation

Take a bite out of estimation with this appetizing activity! Give each youngster a clean apple, and ask him to estimate how many bites it will take for him to eat it. Have him record his response on a sheet of paper. Then ask the student to eat his apple, making a tally mark on his paper after each bite. When each student has finished eating his apple, instruct him to total his tally marks. Have each youngster find the difference between the actual number of bites and his estimate. For more learning fun, challenge each student to name the number of tens and ones in his total or tell whether the total number of bites is odd or even.

## A Tasty Poem

This "a-peeling" booklet project is sure to please! Give each student a white construction-paper copy of page 20. Ask each youngster to personalize and color her booklet cover. Read the poem with your students; then have each youngster illustrate the pages as desired. Next ask each student to cut out her pattern pieces along the bold lines. Have her sequence and lay the cutouts end-to-end. Instruct her to glue the cutouts together where indicated to create one long strip. Using the thin lines as guides, help each youngster accordion-fold the pages as shown. Then encourage each student to take her booklet home to read with family members.

## The Good News Is...

What's so good about an apple tree growing in your stomach? Find out and reinforce critical thinking with this humorous literature-based project. Read aloud to students *What's So Terrible About Swallowing An Apple Seed?* by Harriet Lerner and Susan Goldhor (HarperCollins Publishers, Inc.; 1996). Then discuss the gloomy thoughts Rosie had after she swallowed apple seeds and the fun ideas Katie had about this predicament. On a sheet of chart paper, write "The bad news is…" Then list several story prompts similar to the following:

- My hair glows in the dark!
- The tip of my nose is a lit candle!
- Whenever I open my mouth, it shines like a flashlight!
- I grew a dragon's tail.

Instruct each child to write on a sheet of drawing paper "The bad news is" and complete the sentence with a prompt from the list as shown. Next have her write "The good news is" near the bottom of the page, then write and illustrate the positive side of the situation. Compile and bind students' completed pages into a class book titled "Bad News/Good News." Now that's looking on the bright side!

The bad news is the tip of my nose is a lit candle!

The good news is I don't need lights on at night. I can roast marshmallows when I want them.

A
**Tasty Poem**

**Illustrated by**

_____
Name

Little inchworm, see him go,

Way up high where apples grow.

Glue here.

Slowly, slowly up the tree,

Little inchworm soon you'll see.

Red and green and yellow, too,

Glue here.

Tasty apples just for you!

Yum!

©1999 The Education Center, Inc.

# Bull's-Eye!

Roll a die.
Write the number in a section on the target.
Roll the die two more times to make a three-digit number.
The first one has been done for you.

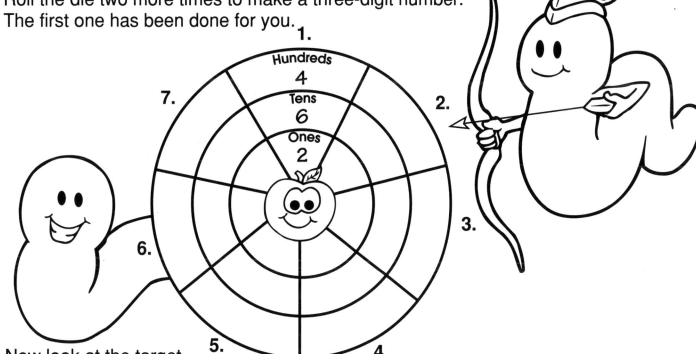

Now look at the target.
Write how many hundreds, tens, and ones.
Then write the number on the line.
The first one has been done for you.

1. __4__ hundreds __6__ tens __2__ ones = ____462____

2. ____ hundreds _____ tens _____ ones = _____

3. ____ hundreds _____ tens _____ ones = _____

4. ____ hundreds _____ tens _____ ones = _____

5. ____ hundreds _____ tens _____ ones = _____

6. ____ hundreds _____ tens _____ ones = _____

7. ____ hundreds _____ tens _____ ones = _____

**Bonus Box:** Rearrange the digits in each problem; then write the new numbers on the back of this sheet. Circle the greatest new number.

**Note To The Teacher:** Each student or pair of students will need a die for this activity.

Name _____

# Rhyme Time!

Cut out the worm cards.
Glue each one to make a rhyming pair.

**1.**
coat

**2.**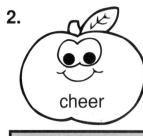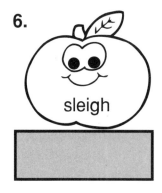
cheer

**3.**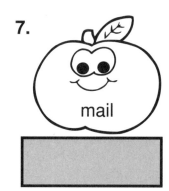
moon

**4.**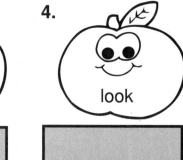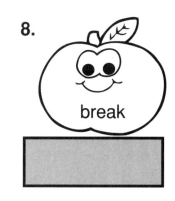
look

**5.**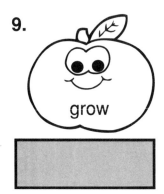
keep

**6.**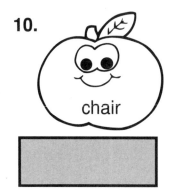
sleigh

**7.**
mail

**8.**
break

**9.**
grow

**10.**
chair

**11.**
brown

**12.**
lunch

**Bonus Box:** Write six more pairs of rhyming words on the back of this sheet.

©1999 The Education Center, Inc. • *September Monthly Reproducibles* • Grades 2–3 • TEC957 • Key p. 63

soon  clown  snow  bunch
steak  float  weigh  book
steer  stair  snail  sleep

Name _____

# Hungry For Math

**Solve each problem.**
**Write the answer on the apple.**

$$\begin{array}{r} 95 \\ -\ 14 \\ \hline \end{array}$$ = I

$$\begin{array}{r} 38 \\ -\ 13 \\ \hline \end{array}$$ = H

$$\begin{array}{r} 98 \\ -\ 34 \\ \hline \end{array}$$ = G

$$\begin{array}{r} 49 \\ -\ 27 \\ \hline \end{array}$$ = W

$$\begin{array}{r} 73 \\ -\ 41 \\ \hline \end{array}$$ = S

$$\begin{array}{r} 67 \\ -\ 10 \\ \hline \end{array}$$ = N

$$\begin{array}{r} 88 \\ -\ 53 \\ \hline \end{array}$$ = O

$$\begin{array}{r} 56 \\ -\ 23 \\ \hline \end{array}$$ = T

$$\begin{array}{r} 81 \\ -\ 60 \\ \hline \end{array}$$ = A

$$\begin{array}{r} 19 \\ -\ 11 \\ \hline \end{array}$$ = N

**To solve the puzzle, write each matching letter on the lines below.**

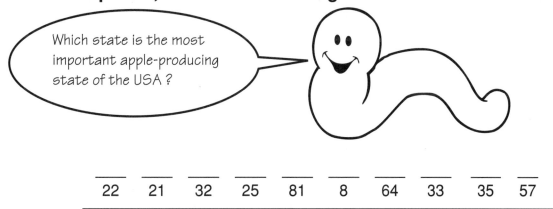

Which state is the most important apple-producing state of the USA ?

___ ___ ___ ___ ___ ___ ___ ___ ___ ___
22  21  32  25  81  8   64  33  35  57

**Bonus Box:** On the back of this sheet, write about one way you like to eat apples.

Name_____

It's Apple Time!
Digraphs: *ch, sh, th, wh*

# It's Apple-Picking Time!

Finish each word inside the apples.
Write the digraph *ch, sh, th,* or *wh* on the blank lines.
Then copy each word inside the matching basket.

**Bonus Box:** Choose one word from each basket. Write a sentence with each word on the back of this sheet.

©1999 The Education Center, Inc. • *September Monthly Reproducibles* • Grades 2–3 • TEC957

# AUTUMN

Celebrate autumn's arrival with this bountiful harvest of fall fun!

### "Unbe-leaf-able" Creatures

Try this "tree-rific" creative-writing project! Take students on a walk outside, and have each youngster collect two or three fallen leaves. When you return to the classroom, have each student arrange and glue his leaves on a sheet of drawing paper to make a creature. Ask him to use a variety of craft supplies—such as crayons, wiggle eyes, buttons, and glue—to add features to it. Instruct each student to write a story about his creature; then give him an opportunity to share his completed work with the class. Now that's a "tree-mendous" way to encourage creativity!

### Fabulous Fall Facts

With this eye-catching display of facts, there's no doubt that fall is in the air! Duplicate a class supply of page 26 on yellow construction paper, and give each youngster one copy. Share the facts shown below, and have students research additional information about fall. Each student writes one fall fact on his lined leaf. Then he colors both leaves, being careful to leave his writing visible. Next he cuts out the leaves and glues them together. Hole-punch the top of each completed leaf and suspend it from the ceiling to create an informative *and* colorful display.

### Autumn Quilt

Students will warm right up to this autumn quilt project! Read with students *Eight Hands Round: A Patchwork Alphabet* by Ann Whitford Paul (HarperCollins Children's Books, 1996), and discuss the origins of the quilt patterns in this book. Then have each youngster make an autumn tints quilt block. To begin, each student folds a nine-inch square of drawing paper in half twice, then unfolds the paper to reveal four equal-size squares. Next she visually divides two opposite corner squares into four smaller sections as shown. Each student illustrates or writes about favorite fall activities in the two large squares. She colors the remaining squares, then glues her completed block onto an 11-inch construction-paper square. Finally, she draws stitch marks along the edges of each section and personalizes her work. Mount students' completed quilt blocks together on a bulletin board or wall to create one large autumn quilt.

My family and I pick apples every fall. Then my mom makes homemade applesauce.

I like to jump into piles of leaves. It's lots of fun!

- Autumn begins on September 22 or 23 in the Northern Hemisphere.
- Autumn is the season when most hurricanes occur.
- The first full moon in autumn is known as the harvest moon.
- When monarch butterflies migrate in autumn, they travel 10 to 15 mph.
- The last day of autumn in the Northern Hemisphere is on or about December 21.

# Patterns

Use with "Fabulous Fall Facts" on page 25.

Name _____

# A Heap Of Nuts

Write **s** or **es** to make each word plural.
Write each plural word on the tree.

Remember, if a word ends in s, sh, ch, x, or z, add es.

bush ___

acorn ___

tree ___

owl ___

fox ___

lunch ___

apple ___

branch ___

pumpkin ___

squirrel ___

buzz ___

basket ___

class ___

squash ___

**Bonus Box:** Choose five of the words listed on the tree. Use them to write a fall story on the back of this sheet.

©1999 The Education Center, Inc. • *September Monthly Reproducibles* • Grades 2–3 • TEC957

27

Name _____

# Fall Fun

Solve each problem.
Write the answer on the leaf.
Use the code to color
    the leaves.

2 x 9 =

5 x 2 =

3 x 3 =

4 x 2 =

3 x 5 =

5 x 5 =

2 x 6 =

5 x 7 =

3 x 4 =

4 x 4 =

4 x 6 =

3 x 7 =

1 x 1 =

**Color Code**
even answer = red

odd answer = orange

**Bonus Box:** Sammy Squirrel catches two leaves each day. How many leaves will he have in seven days? Solve this problem on the back of this sheet.

# Pumpkin Punctuation

Color each pumpkin that shows the missing punctuation.

1. Pumpkins are orange

2. Don't drop the pumpkin

3. Oh my, that pumpkin has a lot of seeds

4. Have you ever been to a pumpkin farm

5. Pumpkin seeds are good to eat

6. Look out for that pumpkin vine

7. Do you like pumpkin pie

8. Pumpkins can grow very large

9. How heavy is that pumpkin

10. Some people carve pumpkins

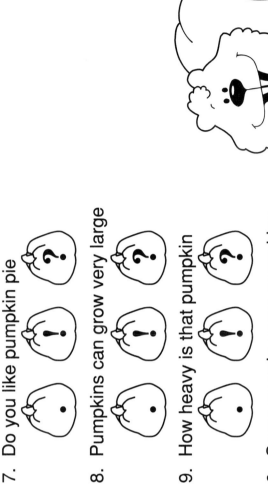

**Bonus Box:** Imagine that you grew the world's biggest pumpkin. On the back of this sheet, write a story about it. Remember to punctuate each sentence.

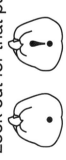

# Falling Numbers

Solve each problem.
Write the answer on the leaf.
Color the leaves by the code.

14
−7

18
−9

12
−4

16
−5

9
−5

16
−8

10
−7

8
−3

14
−9

18
−6

13
−2

15
−8

**Color Code**
answers less than 8 = red
answers greater than 7 = orange

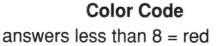

11
−6

17
−4

**Bonus Box:** On the back of this sheet, write two subtraction word problems. Then ask a classmate to solve them.

# Tomie dePaola

Celebrate author Tomie dePaola's September 15 birthday with this festive collection of literature-based activities!

## Dynamite dePaola

Spark students' interest in reading with this dynamite book-sharing idea! In a designated area of your classroom, place a class supply of the book-sharing form on page 32 and several of Tomie dePaola's books (see the titles listed on this page). Each time a student finishes reading one of these books or another book by this author, ask him to complete a book-sharing form. Post his completed sheet near your featured book collection; then have the student review the other forms displayed to help him choose another book. With this spectacular idea, reading time will be a blast!

## Magical Mixtures

No tribute to Tomie dePaola would be complete without a Strega Nona story! For each student, duplicate page 33 and gather the supplies listed on the reproducible. Then share with youngsters a Strega Nona tale (see the titles recommended on this page). Tell students that each of them will create his own "magical" mixture with red, yellow, and blue food coloring. Explain that these colors are *primary* colors and they can be used to create *secondary* colors. Give each student a copy of the reproducible, guide him through the experiment, and then ask him to share his results. Finally, help students determine the combinations of primary colors that resulted in each of their secondary colors.

## What's Cooking?

Follow up "Magical Mixtures" on this page with this eye-catching creative-writing project! In advance, purchase red, blue, and yellow curling ribbon. Give each student a copy of the pattern on page 32. Instruct her to color her cooking pot the same color that resulted from her "Magical Mixtures" experiment, then cut it out. Next have her cut several lengths of ribbon to represent the two primary colors she used. Help the student carefully curl the ribbons with scissors. Then instruct her to glue the ribbon atop her pattern as shown. Have each student write a creative story to accompany her project, such as "The Purple Potion" or "The Outrageous Orange Ooze," and use the decorated cooking pot as a paper topper.

The Purple Potion
Once upon a time, there was a strega who had fantastic magical powers. Every day she mixed a different magic potion in her cooking pot. One day she mixed a

## Recommended Titles By Tomie dePaola

*The Art Lesson* (Paperstar, 1997)
*The Legend Of The Bluebonnet* (Houghton Mifflin Company, 1993)
*The Legend Of The Indian Paintbrush* (Paperstar, 1996)
*Strega Nona* (Simon & Schuster Children's Division, 1997)
*Strega Nona: Her Story* (G. P. Putnam's Sons, 1996)
*Strega Nona Meets Her Match* (Paperstar, 1996)

# Tomie dePaola Is Dynamite!

Title: _____

This book was read by _____

The best part of this book was _____

_____

_____

I think this book     (Color one choice.)

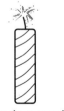                              

needs a spark          had a few sparks          was a blast to read          was dynamite

because _____ .

# Magical Mixtures

Strega Nona has magic in her cooking pot.
Follow the directions to make a "magical" mixture of your own.

**You need:**
1 six-inch plastic plate
about 1/4 cup whole milk
1 toothpick
3–4 drops of dishwashing soap on a
   piece of waxed paper
2 different colors of food coloring (red,
   blue, or yellow)
crayons

 **1** Pour the milk onto the plate.
Add two drops of different-colored
   food coloring.
Draw and color what you see.

 **2** What do you think will happen if you
   add soap?

_____

_____

_____

Draw and color a picture to show
   your prediction.

 **3** Dip the toothpick in the soap.
Hold it in your mixture, and slowly
   count to five.
Remove the toothpick.
Draw and color what you see.

 **4** Repeat the third step, this time plac-
   ing the toothpick in a different spot
   in the milk.
Draw and color what you see.

**Note To The Teacher:** Use with "Magical Mixtures" on page 31.

# Watch Out For Quicksand!

Read or listen to *The Quicksand Book* by Tomie dePaola.
Read the questions.
Look in the book to find the answers.
Write the answers.
Then color the pictures.

1. What is quicksand?
   (page 10)

   _____
   _____
   _____
   _____

2. What should you do if you fall into quicksand?
   (page 13)

   _____
   _____
   _____
   _____
   _____
   _____

3. Where can quicksand be found?
   (pages 16 and 17)

   _____
   _____
   _____
   _____
   _____
   _____
   _____

HELP!

4. How can you watch out for quicksand? (page 20)

   _____
   _____
   _____
   _____
   _____
   _____

5. What is one way to get out of quicksand? (page 23)

   _____
   _____
   _____
   _____
   _____
   _____

**Bonus Box:** What would you take on a trip to the jungle? On the back of this sheet, make a list of at least five things, and explain why you chose them.

**Note To The Teacher:** Introduce this reproducible activity by reading aloud or having each student read *The Quicksand Book* by
Tomie dePaola (Houghton Mifflin Company, 1993).

# NATIONAL STUDENT DAY ™

September 17, National Student Day™, is the perfect time to spotlight students. Use this "dino-mite" collection of awards and activities to honor the youngsters in your class!

## ON THE WAY TO SCHOOL

Some days, getting to school is quite an adventure! There's no doubt your students have plenty of stories to share on this subject. Give each youngster an opportunity to embellish such a story and enjoy the limelight with this creative-writing activity. Read aloud and discuss *The Secret Shortcut* by Mark Teague (Scholastic Inc., 1996). This delightful tale tells about the obstacles Wendell and Floyd face on their way to school. To avoid them, the boys decide to take a shortcut that results in an unbelievable adventure. Have each student invent a shortcut from her home to school, then write and illustrate a story about it. Encourage students to make their routes as outrageous as the one that Wendell and Floyd took. Invite each student to share her completed story; then present an award to her (see pages 37 and 38 for reproducible patterns). Awards may be given for categories, such as the silliest, scariest, longest, or funniest shortcuts.

What was my favorite school lunch?
What subject did I like the most?
What subject did I like the least?
How did I travel to school each day?
Did I ever move to a new school?
What did I like to do during recess?

## ONCE UPON A TIME

Do your students realize that you were once a student, too? Share a bit of your past and learn more about your students with this fun get-acquainted activity. Show students a photo of yourself when you were about their age and tell about a few of your school experiences. Then have each student visually divide a sheet of paper into two columns and label one column with your name and the other with his name. Ask students school-related questions such as the ones shown. Have each student write how he thinks you would answer the questions in the first column, then write his own answers to the same questions in the second column. Share and discuss your answers with youngsters, and ask them to compare and contrast your responses with theirs. Students might be surprised at how much they have in common with you!

I always finish my work on time! Jon

## PEPPY PENNANTS

Boost your students' self-esteem with these personalized pennants! Have youngsters brainstorm characteristics of a great student while you list their ideas on the chalkboard. Then ask each student to choose from the list one quality that describes her. Have the youngster cut out a large triangular-shaped pennant from colored construction paper. On her pennant, instruct each student to write a complete sentence about the quality she chose. Then have her illustrate her pennant with a self-portrait and personalize it as desired. Display the pennants on a bulletin board titled "[Teacher's name] Has Flagged Down Some Super Students!"

# NAME THAT STUDENT!

**Read each clue.**
**Find the matching dinosaur.**
**Write its name on the desk.**

| _____ Dinosaur | _____ Dinosaur | _____ Dinosaur |
|---|---|---|

1. Drew Dinosaur does not have plates.
2. Dee Dinosaur sits beside a dinosaur with a long neck.
3. Don Dinosaur sits between Drew and Dee.

**Cut out each box.**
**Read the clues.**
**Glue each set of clues below the matching dinosaur.**

**Bonus Box:** Choose one of these dinosaurs. On the back of this sheet, write a fantasy story about its day at school.

This dinosaur wears four shoes at recess.

His name is Larry Longneck.

---

Rep Dial has sharp claws.

She shines her plates every day before school.

---

Dino Might's big tail helps him balance when he walks to school.

He uses his sharp teeth to eat a school lunch.

**"Dino-mite"**
**Student Award**
**presented to**

_____

**for**

_____

_____

_____   _____
teacher's signature          date

©1999 The Education Center, Inc. • *September Monthly Reproducibles* • Grades 2–3 • TEC957

**PREHISTORIC PRIZE**
**FOR**
**"DINO-RIFFIC" WORK**
**PRESENTED TO**

_____

_____
teacher's signature

_____
date

©1999 The Education Center, Inc. • *September Monthly Reproducibles* • Grades 2–3 • TEC957

**Note To The Teacher:** Duplicate and present awards to students as desired.

**Student Awards**

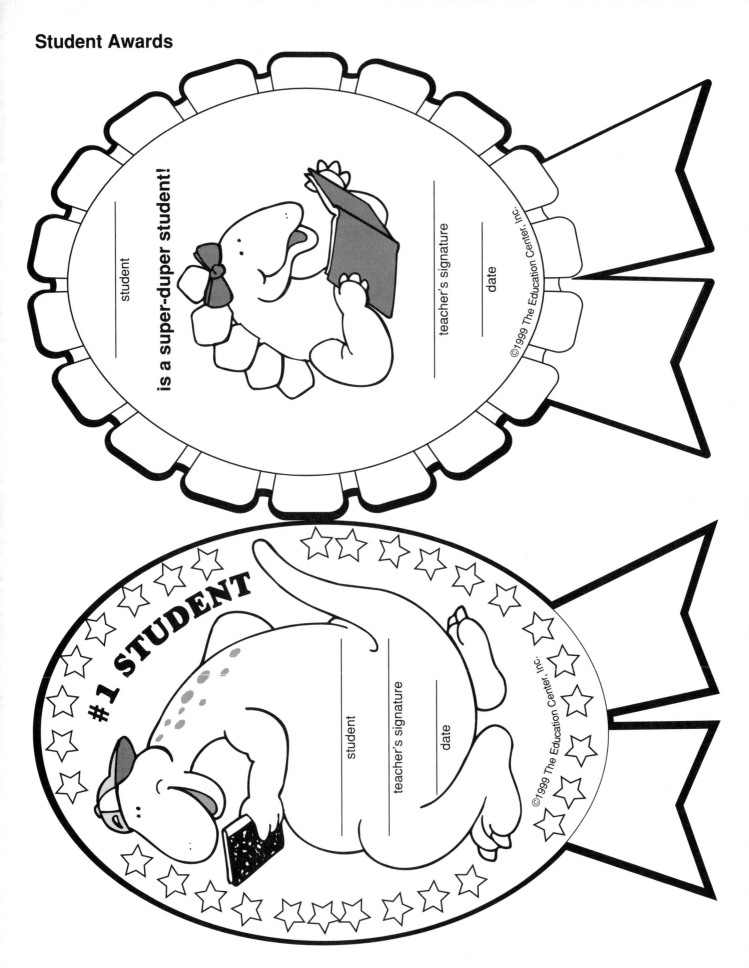

is a super-duper student!

student

teacher's signature

date

©1999 The Education Center, Inc.

#1 STUDENT

student

teacher's signature

date

©1999 The Education Center, Inc.

**Note To The Teacher:** Duplicate and present awards to students as desired.

# ALL EYES ON OWLS

Student learning will soar with these informative activities about the fascinating world of owls!

## Creatures Of The Night

"Whooo" knows what owls do at night? *Your* students will with this owlish booklet activity! Give each student a copy of pages 40–42. Review with youngsters the words in the word bank on page 40. Then read with students the sentences on pages 41 and 42, and have each youngster use the word bank to complete his sentences. Ask each student to personalize the booklet cover and then color his owl and booklet pages as desired. Next have him cut out his owl, booklet cover, and pages; compile his cover and pages in order; and then staple them atop his word bank where indicated. After completing this information-packed booklet, you can be sure that students will be all the wiser!

| Type Of Owl | Special Characteristic | Feathers | Environment | Reproduction | Food | Behavior |
|---|---|---|---|---|---|---|
| Barn Owl | almost white face | speckled feathers and white underside | usually lives in a barn, a cave, a tree, or an old building | lays 4–6 round, white eggs | rodents, sparrows, insects, and frogs | hunts at night |
| Long-Eared Owl | tufts of feathers that look like ears | speckled feathers and grayish-brown underside | lives in a tree at the edge of a forest | lays 3–7 round, white eggs | rodents, birds, insects, and frogs | hunts at night |
| Pygmy Owl | smallest type of owl | brown feathers with spots and white underside | lives in a hollow tree | lays 4–6 small, white, oval eggs | rodents, insects, and small birds | hunts during the day and evening |

## Fine-Feathered Comparisons

This owl fact-sorting activity is beyond compare! On the chalkboard or a sheet of bulletin-board paper, create a chart similar to the one shown. Review the information with students. Then have each youngster choose two of the listed owls to feature in a Venn diagram. Instruct her to draw on a sheet of paper two overlapping circles and label each circle with the name of a selected owl. Next have her write facts about the owls in the appropriate sections of the resulting Venn diagram, referring to the chart as she works. Then group students who worked with the same types of owls. Have each group analyze its diagrams and write three or more sentences about them. For added learning fun, challenge each student to create a Venn diagram that features all three owls.

### Barn Owl | Pygmy Owl

- hunts at night
- round eggs
- eats frogs
- almost white face

**eats rodents, insects, and sparrows**
**white underside**
**lays 4–6 white eggs**

- hunts during the day and evening
- the smallest owl
- oval eggs

**Booklet Owl Pattern**
Use with "Creatures Of The Night" on page 39.

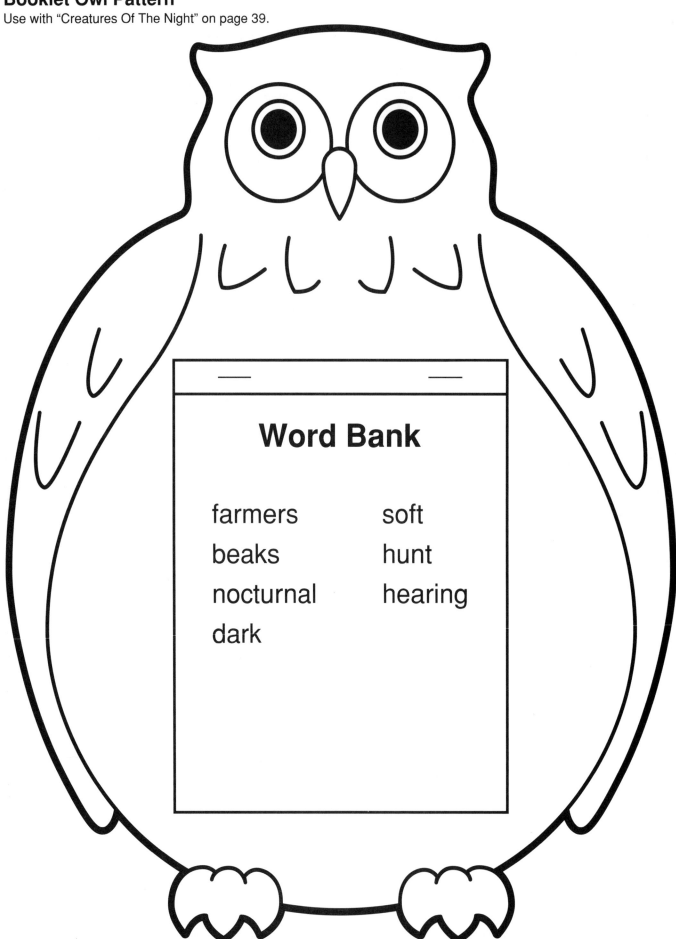

# Word Bank

farmers        soft

beaks          hunt

nocturnal      hearing

dark

# Creatures Of The Night

Name _____

Most owls are _____.
They sleep during the day and
are active at night.

From dusk to dawn, owls
_____ other animals,
such as frogs, lizards, snakes,
and mice.

Owls have many traits that
make them good hunters. For
example, they have hooked
_____, strong
claws, and excellent eyesight.

Owls can see farther than people can. They can see well in the _____, too.

4

Owls' feathers have _____ edges. These special feathers help owls fly very quietly so they can surprise their prey.

5

Owls have a very good sense of _____. They can hear a mouse from about 60 feet away!

6

By hunting mice and other rodents, owls help _____. Without owls, rodents would soon overrun farms.

7

# Cracking Compounds

Help Ollie Owl put the eggs together.
Find each pair of words that can make a compound word.
Color their shells the same color.
Write the compound word on Ollie's paper.

Name _____

# Addition Is A Hoot!

Solve each problem.
Write the answer on the
feather.

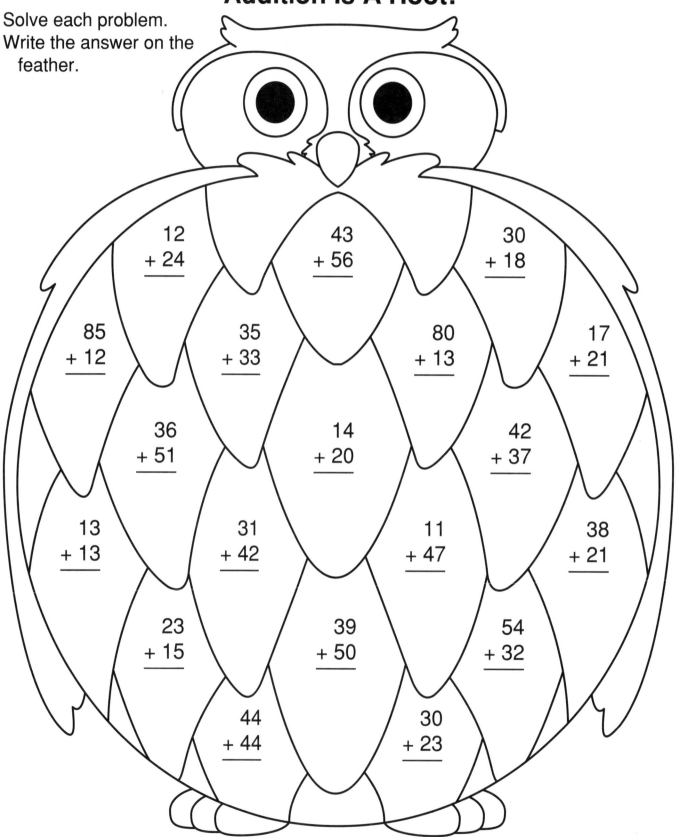

12
+ 24
____

43
+ 56
____

30
+ 18
____

85
+ 12
____

35
+ 33
____

80
+ 13
____

17
+ 21
____

36
+ 51
____

14
+ 20
____

42
+ 37
____

13
+ 13
____

31
+ 42
____

11
+ 47
____

38
+ 21
____

23
+ 15
____

39
+ 50
____

54
+ 32
____

44
+ 44
____

30
+ 23
____

**Bonus Box:** Color each feather with an even answer brown. Color each feather with an odd answer yellow.
Color the rest of the owl any way that you choose.

# ALL-AMERICAN
# BREAKFAST MONTH

Mark your calendars! September is All-American Breakfast Month. These appetizing activities and reproducibles are made-to-order for a hearty helping of learning fun!

## Eggs Over Easy

This fast-paced relay game is sure to generate lots of "egg-citement"! In advance, obtain four empty egg cartons and two dozen plastic eggs. Label each of 24 slips of paper with a different breakfast word; then place one slip inside each egg. To play the game, divide the class into two equal teams. Have the students on each team line up, one behind the other. Place an egg carton filled with the prepared eggs in front of the first child in each line, and an empty carton behind the last child. At your signal, each egg must be passed alternately over the head and between the knees of each child in line as quickly as possible. The last child in each line must then place the egg in the carton behind her. Once the eggs have been transferred to the empty carton, have each team open their eggs, read the words on the slips of paper, and place them in ABC order on a designated work surface. The first team to successfully transfer all of their eggs and correctly alphabetize their words wins!

### Breakfast Menu

1 bowl toasted oats
1/2 cup milk
3 strawberry slices
1/2 cup orange juice
1 slice of cheese

Fats, Oils, and Sweets (Use sparingly)

Dairy (2-3 servings) | Protein (2-3 servings)

Vegetables (3-5 servings) | Fruits (2-4 servings)

Grains (6-11 servings)

## Well-Balanced Meals

Reinforce the importance of eating a healthful breakfast with this menu-planning activity. Draw and label a large Food Guide Pyramid on the chalkboard (see the illustration). Review with students the parts of the pyramid and the recommended number of servings for each food group. Then name several different breakfast foods, and have students identify the food group to which each one belongs. List youngsters' responses on the pyramid in the appropriate sections. Next have each student create, write, and illustrate on a sheet of drawing paper a menu for a healthful breakfast. Remind her to include nutritious items from each food group. Ask each student to share her completed menu with a classmate and challenge the classmate to identify the food group represented by each food. Then encourage each youngster to try her menu at home with her family's assistance.

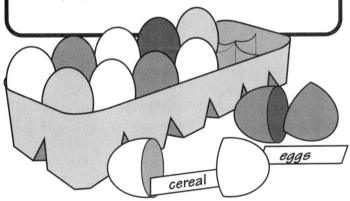

cereal

eggs

## Breakfast Bonanza

What better way to celebrate All-American Breakfast Month than with a Breakfast Bonanza? After your students understand the importance of eating a well-balanced meal each morning, schedule a classroom breakfast. Several days in advance, enlist parent help by sending home with each student a copy of the letter on page 46. On the morning of the bonanza, prepare a table buffet style with paper plates, bowls, napkins, cups, and plastic utensils. When the children arrive, add their breakfast foods to the table. As students enjoy their meals, invite youngsters to identify the benefits of eating a nutritious breakfast. After the breakfast, give each student a copy of the thank-you note on page 46. Have him cut out his note, fold it in half, and write a personal note of thanks on the inside for the contribution his family made to the breakfast. Ask youngsters to hand deliver the notes to their families. Now, that's a meal that will leave everyone feeling satisfied!

**Patterns**

Dear Parent,

In celebration of All-American Breakfast Month, our class will be having a Breakfast Bonanza on _____. If you are able to contribute one of the items on the list below, please complete this slip and return it to school with your child by _____.

date

Thank you for your help!

date

_____
teacher's signature

My child, _____, will bring

☐ orange juice    ☐ bagels         ☐ bananas
☐ milk           ☐ cream cheese   ☐ strawberries
☐ dry cereal     ☐ jelly           ☐ blueberries
☐ muffins       ☐ butter         ☐ grapefruit

to the Breakfast Bonanza on _____.

date

_____
parent's signature

©1999 The Education Center, Inc. • *September Monthly Reproducibles* • Grades 2–3 • TEC957

Breakfast Bonanza

Thank You for your contribution to our Breakfast Bonanza!

©1999 The Education Center, Inc.

   **Note To The Teacher:** Use with "Breakfast Bonanza" on page 45.

Name _____

# Rise And Shine!

**Read the story.**

Jill and Jody tiptoe into the kitchen. The sun is just coming up outside. Jill goes to the refrigerator and takes out two eggs and some bacon. She begins to cook them in a frying pan. Jody pours a tall glass of orange juice. Then she puts some bread in the toaster.

Pop! Up comes the toast. "Good timing!" whispers Jill. "The eggs and bacon are ready, too."

The girls place everything neatly on a tray. Then Jill carries the tray through the hall. "I hope Mom is surprised," says Jody.

"Rise and shine!" they shout. Mom rubs her eyes and smiles at the girls' surprise.

**Answer the questions.**

1. What time of day is it? _____

2. Why do Jill and Jody tiptoe and whisper? _____

_____

3. What is the girls' surprise? _____

_____

4. What do you think Mom will do now? _____

_____

5. What might be another good title for this story? _____

_____

**Draw and color three pictures to show the beginning, middle, and end of the story.**

| | | |
|---|---|---|
| | | |

Name _____

# Mixed-Up Menu

Cut out the menu items at the bottom of the page.
Place three menu items on the placemat to make a meal.
Use a breakfast choice, a side order, and a beverage.

What is the breakfast choice?

_____

What is the side order?

_____

What is the beverage?

_____

**Use the cutouts to make 11 more different breakfasts and complete the chart.**

|          | Breakfast Choice | Side Order | Beverage |
|----------|------------------|------------|----------|
| meal #1  |                  |            |          |
| meal #2  |                  |            |          |
| meal #3  |                  |            |          |
| meal #4  |                  |            |          |
| meal #5  |                  |            |          |
| meal #6  |                  |            |          |
| meal #7  |                  |            |          |
| meal #8  |                  |            |          |
| meal #9  |                  |            |          |
| meal #10 |                  |            |          |
| meal #11 |                  |            |          |
| meal #12 |                  |            |          |

©1999 The Education Center, Inc. • *September Monthly Reproducibles* • Grades 2–3 • TEC957 • Key p. 64

- - - - - - - - - - - - - - - - - - - - - - - - - - - - - - - - - - - - -

<u>Breakfast Choices</u>     <u>Side Orders</u>   <u>Beverages</u>

48

# Ice Cream Month

On September 22, 1903, Italo Marchiony applied for a patent for the ice-cream cone. Celebrate his tasty accomplishment by dishing up these mouthwatering activities and reproducibles!

*Follow the rules.*

*Take turns.*

*Do all of your homework on time.*

Alyssa
Name

## Appetizing Advice

Set the stage for a great school year with this student-made back-to-school display! Give each student a copy of page 50. Have her write one tip for having a successful school year on each scoop. Then ask the youngster to very lightly color her scoops and cone as desired, being careful to leave her writing visible. Have each student cut out her patterns, then glue the scoops atop her cone as shown. Display youngsters' completed ice-cream cones on a brightly colored bulletin board titled "Good Advice By The Gallon."

## Here's The Scoop!

Students will get the scoop on column addition with this irresistible center! Make nine ice-cream-scoop cutouts and 19 cone cutouts from construction paper (use the patterns on page 50 if desired). Label each scoop with a different numeral from 1 to 9. Label each cone with a different numeral from 6 to 24. Then cut out 24 small red construction-paper circles. If desired, laminate all of the cutouts for durability. Place the cutouts in an ice-cream container in a center. To use the center, a student assembles ice-cream cones, each with three scoops and a cone. To determine the correct cone for each set of scoops, the student adds the numerals on the scoops and matches their sum with the numeral on a cone. Encourage her to use the red "cherries" as manipulatives to check her answers. Now, that's an addition idea that students will eat up!

Ice-Cream Pizza
Cost: $6.95

sugar cookie

vanilla ice cream

strawberries

This pizza is both creamy and crunchy! It's easy to serve because it comes in slices.
Name Charles

## Ice-Cream Dreams

Entice your students to think creatively with this tantalizing persuasive-writing activity! Have students brainstorm ice-cream treats and list their ideas on the chalkboard. Then direct each student to invent a new treat, referring to the brainstormed list for ideas. Have the student design on a sheet of drawing paper an advertisement promoting his ice-cream concoction. Instruct him to include in his ad a description of his ice-cream treat and other information that he thinks would persuade someone to buy his product. Bind students' completed ads between construction-paper covers, and title the resulting book "Ice-Cream Dreams." Read the book with students. Then ask each youngster to name a treat that he would like to buy and explain his reason for selecting it. What a tasty approach to persuasive writing!

# Patterns

Use with "Appetizing Advice" and "Here's The Scoop!" on page 49.

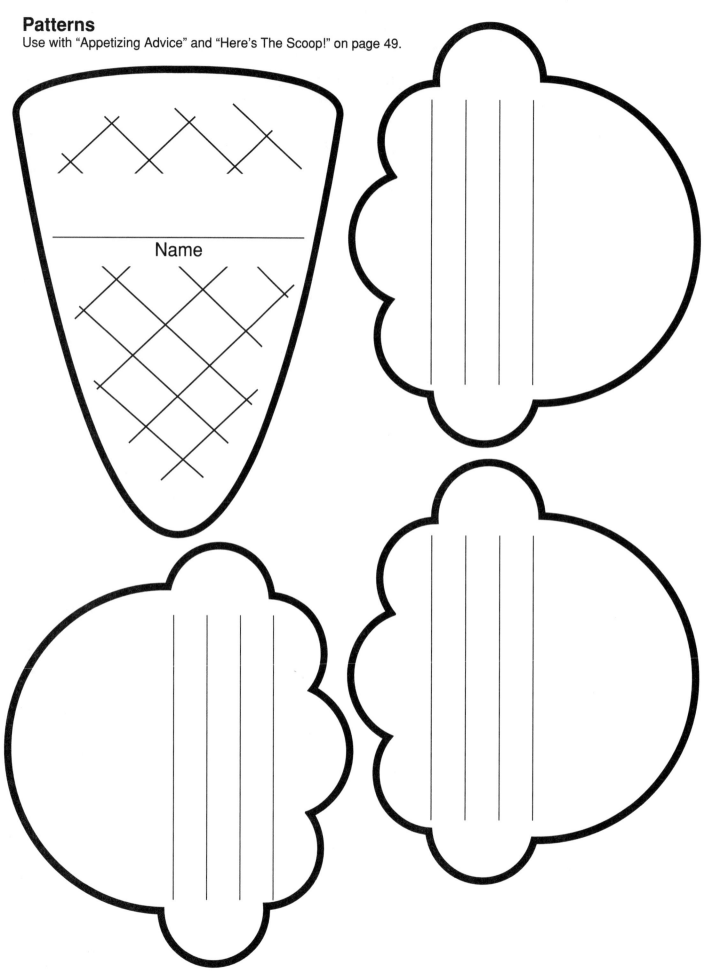

Name

Name _____

# Double The Fun

Cut out the scoops at the bottom of this sheet. Glue each scoop onto an ice-cream cone to equal the total cost shown.

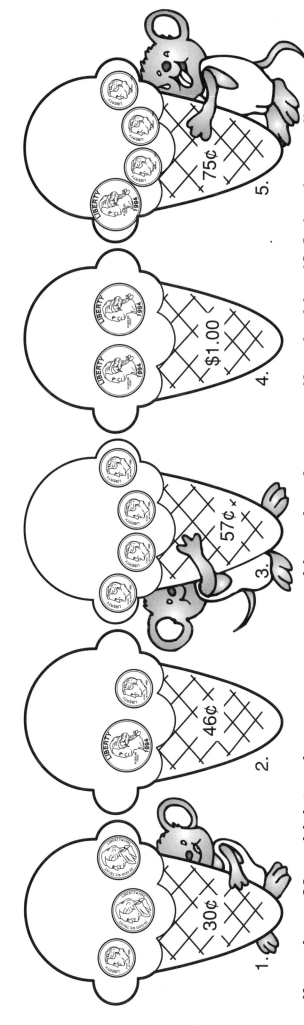

1. 30¢

2. 46¢

3. 57¢

4. $1.00

5. 75¢

**If you have 80¢, which two ice-cream cones could you buy for yourself and a friend? Color them yellow.**

**Bonus Box:** If you bought cone #5 with $1.00, how much change would you get? Write your answer on the back of this sheet.

©1999 The Education Center, Inc. • *September Monthly Reproducibles* • Grades 2–3 • TEC957 • Key p. 64

# We Scream For Ice Cream!

Complete each word on the ice cream.
Write the blend *br, cr, dr,* or *gr* on the lines.
Use the code to color each ice-cream scoop.

_____ owd

_____ ade

_____ aw

_____ ive

_____ um

_____ anch

_____ ight

_____ aid

_____ agon

_____ een

_____ ust

_____ eat

_____ ack

_____ ing

_____ ib

## Color Code

**br** = brown   **cr** = pink   **dr** = yellow   **gr** = purple

**Bonus Box:** On the back of this sheet, write three more words that begin with *gr.*

©1999 The Education Center, Inc. • *September Monthly Reproducibles* • Grades 2–3 • TEC957

Name_____

# Fabulous Flavors

Write the words on each bowl in ABC order.

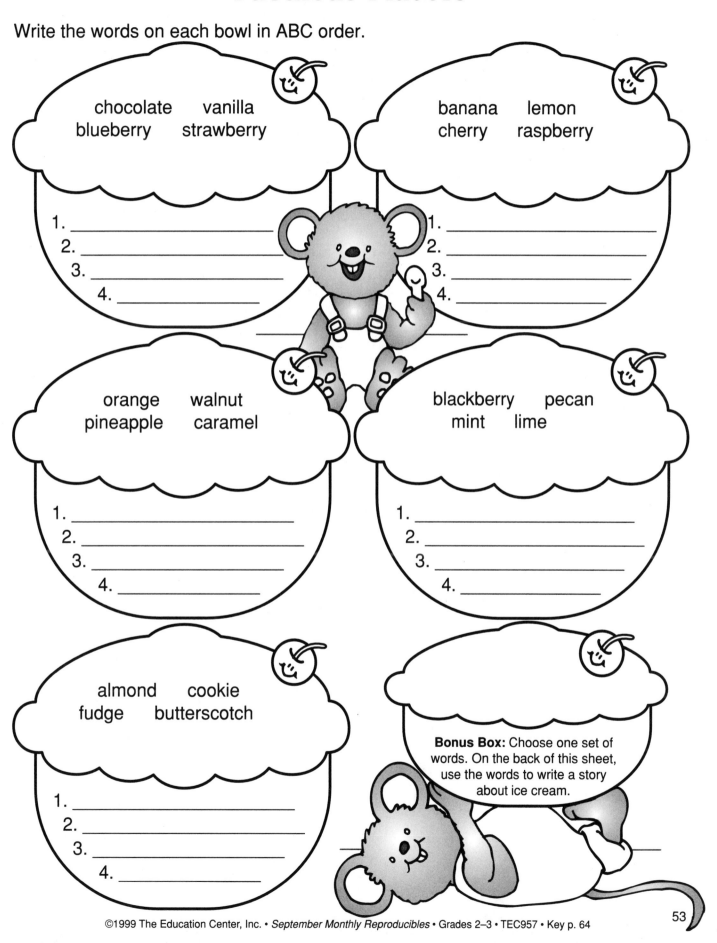

chocolate    vanilla
blueberry    strawberry

1. _____
2. _____
3. _____
4. _____

banana    lemon
cherry    raspberry

1. _____
2. _____
3. _____
4. _____

orange    walnut
pineapple    caramel

1. _____
2. _____
3. _____
4. _____

blackberry    pecan
mint    lime

1. _____
2. _____
3. _____
4. _____

almond    cookie
fudge    butterscotch

1. _____
2. _____
3. _____
4. _____

**Bonus Box:** Choose one set of words. On the back of this sheet, use the words to write a story about ice cream.

©1999 The Education Center, Inc. • *September Monthly Reproducibles* • Grades 2–3 • TEC957 • Key p. 64

Name _____

# Super-Duper Scoops

For each set of treats, read how much one scoop costs.
Count the scoops.
Write the total cost for each ice-cream treat.
Two have been done for you.

# NATIONAL
# CHICKEN MONTH

Take wing with these Grade A activities and reproducibles during September, National Chicken Month!

## Chicken Challenge

Here's an "egg-cellent" way for your youngsters to practice basic math skills! Make several copies of page 56 on light-colored construction paper. Program each chicken and egg pair with different word problems that have the same answer (see the illustration). Then cut out the programmed chickens and eggs, and label the backs of them for self-checking. Laminate the pieces for durability if desired. In a learning center, place the prepared cutouts in a basket. To use the center, a student solves the problem on a chicken. She then finds the egg that has a problem with the same answer. She turns over both cutouts to check her work. The student continues in a like manner until she has paired all of the cutouts correctly. For a fun language arts variation, program each chicken with a word and each corresponding egg with a synonym for that word.

I just found a golden egg! Guess what I'm going to do with it.

Have you heard about the chicken that laid the golden egg? It looks like...

My golden egg is starting to crack. Oh, my! I see...

Charlie Chicken won 28 ribbons at the fair. He gave 13 of them to his friend. How many ribbons does Charlie have now?

Eggbert Egg has 8 friends who live in Eggville. He has 7 more friends who live in Yolkdale. How many friends does Eggbert have in all?

## Golden Writing Opportunities

Looking for a nifty creative-writing idea? If so, this activity is "eggs-actly" what you're searching for! Enlarge and copy a class supply of an egg pattern on page 56; then give a copy to each student. Next have each youngster use one of the story starters shown to write a story on his egg. After he has completed his story, ask him to lightly color his egg yellow. Have the student cut it out and glue it onto a slightly larger piece of yellow construction paper. Instruct him to trim the project to leave an even construction-paper border around his egg. Then display the golden eggs on a brightly colored bulletin board titled " 'Eggs-traordinary' Eggs!"

## Books To Cluck Over

*The Painter Who Loved Chickens* by Olivier Dunrea (Farrar, Straus & Giroux, Inc.; 1995)
*Chickie Riddles* by Katy Hall and Lisa Eisenberg (Dial Books For Young Readers, 1997)
*When Chickens Grow Teeth: A Story From The French Of Guy de Maupassant* retold by Wendy Anderson Halperin (Orchard Books, 1996)
*Chicken Little* retold by Steven Kellogg (Mulberry Books, 1987)

# Patterns

Use with "Chicken Challenge" and "Golden Writing Opportunities" on page 55.

# Vowel "Eggs-travaganza"

Cut out the eggs.
Read the word on each egg.
Glue each egg below the matching chicken.

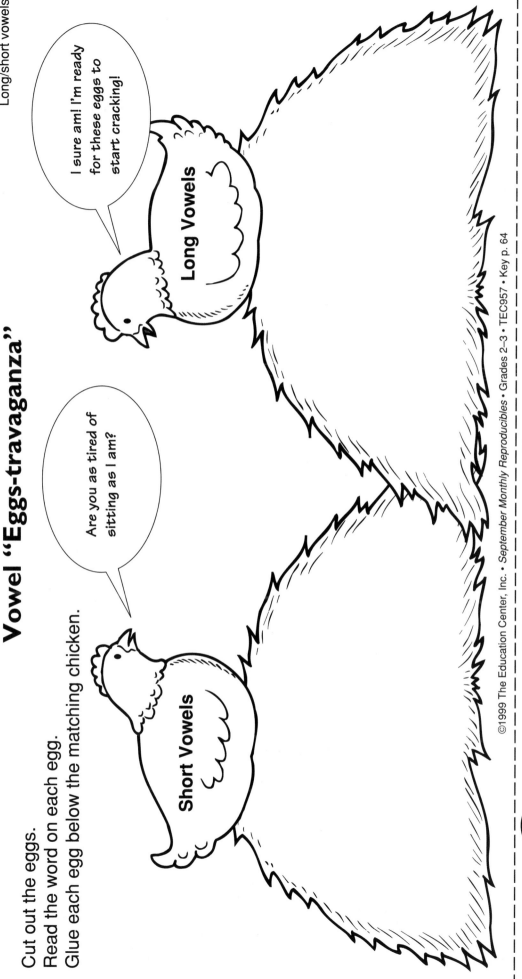

Are you as tired of sitting as I am?

**Short Vowels**

I sure am! I'm ready for these eggs to start cracking!

**Long Vowels**

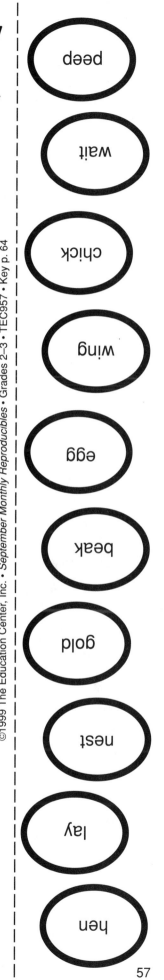

peep

wait

chick

wing

egg

beak

gold

nest

lay

hen

# Chicken "Eggs-press"

Correct each address.
Circle each letter that should be capitalized.
Use the code to decorate the stamp.

Chandra Chicken
805 Poultry parkway
noodle Soup, ohio 42351

Celia Chicken
3 Coop Place
rooster, Iowa 49560

Candace Chicken
317 Feather freeway
Corn country, maine 07563

Cam Chicken
96 Egg Avenue
drumstick, New Mexico
87401

Chuck Chicken
22 loft way
Barnton, Oklahoma 12466

Callie Chicken
101 farm Street
red Crest, Idaho 76002

Cindy Chicken
5 Yolk Drive
peep Point, Kentucky 11121

charlie Chicken
150 Fowl lane
Eggsboro, oregon 97549

Chris chicken
4406 Chick way
Barbecue, New York 36211

cassie Chicken
32 Cluck Court
biscuit City, texas 12443

Chance chicken
20 barnyard Boulevard
nestville, Wisconsin 36008

Cathy Chicken
77 nest Road
Cluck Cluck, Utah 84602

Cody Chicken
111 bird Circle
farmsdale, colorado 88762

**Stamp Code:**
If the envelope has…
**one** missing capital,
**cancel** the stamp.

**two** missing capitals,
**cross out** the stamp.

**three** missing capitals,
**color** the stamp.

Henny Penny
187 Beak Street
Dumpling, Texas 90210

# National Honey Month

September is National Honey Month. Tickle some taste buds with this timely tribute to honey!

### From Flower To Honey

Most people know that bees make honey, but *how* they make it is a mystery to many. Clear up this mystery for your students with this informative reproducible activity. First read aloud a book that describes how honey is made, such as *The Honey Makers* by Gail Gibbons (Morrow Junior Books, 1997) or *The Magic School Bus Inside A Beehive* by Joanna Cole (Scholastic Inc., 1996). Then, with students' help, summarize the honey-making process and list the steps on the chalkboard as shown. Next give each student a copy of page 60. Have him refer to the listed steps to complete his sheet as directed; then challenge him to complete the Bonus Box activity. Now, that's a honey of a lesson!

How Honey Is Made

A worker bee
1. *collects nectar from flowers*
2. *stores it in its honey stomach*
3. *takes the nectar to its hive*
4. *passes the nectar to other bees*

The bees
1. *store the nectar in a honey cell*
2. *fan the nectar*
3. *seal the cell with wax*

The nectar slowly changes into honey.

## A Sweet Center

Put a sweet spin on parts-of-speech practice with this learning center activity! Ask each student to bring from home a recipe that uses honey, and have him copy it onto a large index card. Or, if you prefer, write a few of your favorite honey recipes on separate cards. Place the recipes in a basket or recipe box in a learning center with a supply of blank writing paper. To use the center, a student selects a recipe and copies it onto a sheet of paper. He then underlines each verb with a red crayon and each noun with a blue crayon. After his work has been verified, encourage him to try the recipe at home. For a fun math extension, provide measuring cups and a container of uncooked rice. Have each student use these supplies to determine the amount of each ingredient needed for a double recipe.

### Honey Snacks

(Makes about 30 cookies)

**Ingredients:**
1/2 cup powdered sugar
1/2 cup honey
1/2 cup peanut butter
1 1/2 cups crispy rice cereal
1/2 cup raisins
1/2 cup flaked coconut

Combine the powdered sugar, honey, and peanut butter in a medium-sized bowl. Stir in the cereal and raisins. Shape the dough into one-inch balls. Roll each ball in coconut and place it on a cookie sheet lined with waxed paper. Refrigerate the snacks for one hour or until they are firm to the touch. The snacks may be stored in a tightly covered container in the refrigerator.

### Tasty Treats

Each of your students is sure to develop a sweet tooth as she learns about honey, so count on this no-bake recipe to be a hit! Prepare the recipe shown with students' help. Then as students sample the snacks, share a related story such as *The Bee Tree* by Patricia Polacco (The Putnam Publishing Group, 1993) or a chapter or two from *Winnie-The-Pooh* by A. A. Milne (Puffin Books, 1992).

# From Flower To Honey

Complete each sentence.
Use the Word Bank.
Then write a numeral in each hive to show the correct order.

The bee stores the nectar in its honey _____.

The bees seal the cell with _____.

The bee takes the nectar back to its _____.

First a worker bee collects _____ from flowers.

The nectar slowly changes into _____.

Some bees _____ their wings to help the nectar dry.

The bee passes the nectar to other bees. Then it is stored in a honey cell to _____.

**Word Bank**

honey
fan     dry
hive     wax
stomach     nectar

**Bonus Box:** Imagine that you are a worker bee. On the back of this sheet, write a story about your day.

Name _____

# Busy Bees

Read each sentence.
Write the missing word in the puzzle.
Use the Word Bank.

**Bonus Box**
Would you like
to be a beekeeper?
On the back of
this sheet, explain
why or why not.

1. _____ are helpful insects.

2. A bee lives in a _____.

3. Only one _____ bee lives in the hive.

4. The _____ bees guard the hive.

5. Bees give us _____.

6. The honey is stored in _____ in the hive.

7. Grains of _____ from flowers stick to bees' legs.

8. All bee food comes from _____.

9. The sweet liquid in flowers is called _____ .

10. Bees sure have a _____ job!

**Word Bank**

| | |
|---|---|
| honey | pollen |
| hive | flowers |
| bees | queen |
| sweet | worker |
| cells | nectar |

Name _____

# A Sweet Treat

Read each sentence.
If the sentence is complete, color the honey jar yellow.
If the sentence is incomplete, color the honey jar brown.

    1. Honey is good to eat.

 2. I like to put honey on bread.

 3. Muffins and biscuits, too.

4. I put honey in my oatmeal.

 5. Like it on toast.

 6. Good on pancakes, too.

 7. My mother bakes with honey.

 8. Uses it to make cookies.

 9. And sometimes cakes.

10. Honey-baked ham is a real treat.

 11. Good in lots of foods.

12. I'm glad bees make honey!

**Bonus Box:** On another sheet of paper, rewrite each incomplete sentence to make it complete.

# Answer Keys

## Page 8

Bonus Box: 99, 97, 66, 53, 52, 48, 43, 26, 16, 15, 14, 7, 3

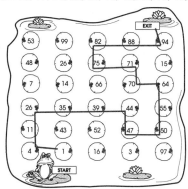

1  4  11  26  35  39  44  47  50
55  64  70  71  75  82  88  94

## Page 9

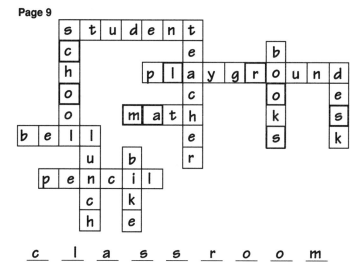

c l a s s r o o m

## Page 10

Complete Sentences:
Flies are buzzing everywhere.
One toad is carrying books.
The toads will learn at school.
Three toads hop to school.
Tom Toad is carrying his bookbag on his back.
One toad brought his lunch.

## Page 13

| Fact | Opinion | |
|---|---|---|
| J | W | 1. Labor Day is celebrated the first Monday in September. |
| I | Q | 2. Labor Day is a fun holiday. |
| N | D | 3. There are many different kinds of jobs. |
| G | B | 4. A firefighter's job is exciting. |
| X | T | 5. A librarian works with books. |
| A | K | 6. It is fun for teachers to work with children. |
| S | V | 7. A doctor's job is more important than a nurse's job. |
| L | P | 8. The president's job is harder than any other job. |
| U | R | 9. Some workers provide goods, and some workers provide services. |
| C | Y | 10. Bakers provide goods like cakes and cookies. |
| M | E | 11. A hairstylist provides a service. |
| F | H | 12. Workers are different in many ways, but they all love Labor Day. |

I T   A L W A Y S
2 5   6 8 1 6 10 7

G E T S   F I R E D !
4 11 5 7   12 2 9 11 3

## Page 14

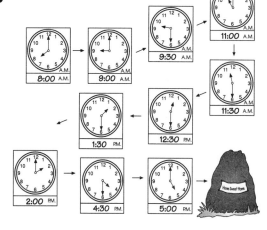

## Page 17

1. east
2. forest
3. west
4. south
5. Main Street and School Street
6. Oak Street and Main Street

**Bonus Box:** Go north on School Street. Turn west onto Main Street. Continue on Main Street until reaching Park Street. Turn right. The hospital is on the left, after the restaurant. (Answers will vary. Accept any reasonable responses.)

## Page 18

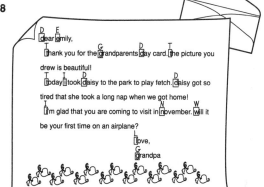

Answers to the questions may vary. Accept any reasonable responses.
1. He thanked her in his letter. He said that the picture was beautiful too.
2. Daisy is a dog. Grandpa wrote about playing fetch with Daisy.
3. Emily will travel to Grandpa's on a plane. They do not live close to each other.

## Page 22

1. float
2. steer
3. soon
4. book
5. sleep
6. weigh
7. snail
8. steak
9. snow
10. stair
11. clown
12. bunch

## Page 23

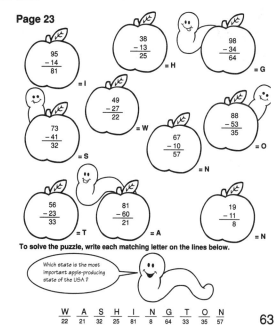

$$95 - 14 = 81 \quad = I$$
$$38 - 13 = 25 \quad = H$$
$$98 - 34 = 64 \quad = G$$
$$49 - 27 = 22 \quad = W$$
$$73 - 41 = 32 \quad = S$$
$$67 - 10 = 57 \quad = N$$
$$88 - 53 = 35 \quad = O$$
$$56 - 23 = 33 \quad = T$$
$$81 - 60 = 21 \quad = A$$
$$19 - 11 = 8 \quad = N$$

To solve the puzzle, write each matching letter on the lines below.

Which state is the most important apple-producing state of the USA ?

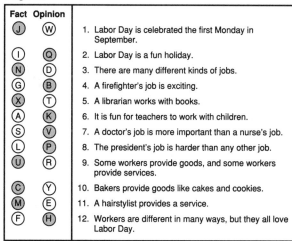

W A S H I N G T O N
22 21 32 25 81 8 64 33 35 57

63

# Answer Keys

## Page 34
(Accept any reasonable responses.)
1. Quicksand is sand that has swelled because water has been forced upward.
2. You should stay calm if you fall in quicksand.
3. Quicksand can be found along shores and in the beds of slow rivers and streams with underground springs.
4. Test the sand with a long stick or pole. The sand will roll like waves if it's quicksand.
5. Lie on your back and put a stick under your shoulders. Push the stick to your hips and slowly pull your legs out. Roll onto the ground.

## Page 36

## Page 41
page 1: nocturnal
page 2: hunt
page 3: beaks

## Page 42
page 4: dark
page 5: soft
page 6: hearing
page 7: farmers

## Page 43
Order of answers may vary.
baseball
nighttime
treetop
pancake
sunlight
eggshell
birdhouse
watermelon
railroad

## Page 47
1. morning
2. Mom is sleeping. They do not want to wake her up.
3. They made breakfast for Mom.
4. Accept any reasonable responses.
5. Accept any reasonable responses.

## Page 48
The order of answers may vary.
meal #1: eggs, bacon, orange juice
meal #2: eggs, sausage, orange juice
meal #3: eggs, bacon, milk
meal #4: eggs, sausage, milk
meal #5: pancakes, bacon, orange juice
meal #6: pancakes, sausage, orange juice
meal #7: pancakes, bacon, milk
meal #8: pancakes, sausage, milk
meal #9: French toast, bacon, orange juice
meal #10: French toast, sausage, orange juice
meal #11: French toast, bacon, milk
meal #12: French toast, sausage, milk

## Page 57
Short Vowels: hen, nest, egg, wing, chick
Long Vowels: lay, gold, beak, wait, peep

## Page 53
blueberry
chocolate
strawberry
vanilla

caramel
orange
pineapple
walnut

almond
butterscotch
cookie
fudge

banana
cherry
lemon
raspberry

blackberry
lime
mint
pecan

## Page 61
1. bees
2. hive
3. queen
4. worker
5. honey
6. cells
7. pollen
8. flowers
9. nectar
10. sweet

## Page 62
1. complete
2. complete
3. incomplete
4. complete
5. incomplete
6. incomplete
7. complete
8. incomplete
9. incomplete
10. complete
11. incomplete
12. complete

## Page 51
Ice-cream cones #1 and #2 should be colored yellow.
Bonus Box: 25¢

## Page 54
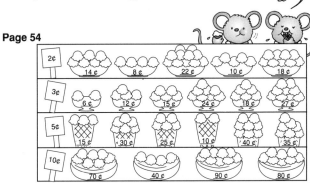

## Page 58

## Page 60
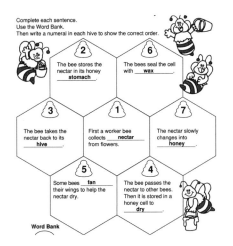